DIGITAL AND INFORMATION LITERACY ™

TWEETING
WITH A PURPOSE

TAMRA B. ORR

rosen publishing's
rosen
central®

New York

Published in 2018 by The Rosen Publishing Group, Inc.
29 East 21st Street, New York, NY 10010

Library of Congress Cataloging-in-Publication Data

Names: Orr, Tamra, author.
Title: Tweeting with a purpose / Tamra B. Orr.
Description: New York : Rosen Central, 2018 | Series: Digital and information literacy | Includes bibliographical references and index. | Audience: Grades 5–8.
Identifiers: LCCN 2017018814| ISBN 9781499439175 (library bound) | ISBN 9781499439151 (pbk.) | ISBN 9781499439168 (6 pack)
Subjects: LCSH: Twitter. | Microblogs. | Social networks.
Classification: LCC HM743.T95 O77 2018 | DDC 302.3—dc23
LC record available at https://lccn.loc.gov/201701881

Manufactured in China

CONTENTS

	Introduction	4
Chapter 1	Friends, Family, and Fun	7
Chapter 2	Keeping Current	16
Chapter 3	Creating Community	24
Chapter 4	Promoting You	32
	Glossary	39
	For More Information	40
	For Further Reading	42
	Bibliography	43
	Index	46

INTRODUCTION

In today's world, emails have replaced hand-written letters, while texting has largely replaced phone calls. Social media posts have replaced face-to-face discussions. So it really is little surprise that a program that takes messages and condenses them to a mere 140 characters is popular. With Twitter, you can stay in touch with your friends, update your family, follow news stories, send messages to your favorite celebrities, and keep track of the companies you care about.

Twitter arrived a couple of years after the creation of similar social networks like Facebook. It went through several names before landing on its now well-known moniker. One dictionary definition of its name is "a short burst of inconsequential information." As founder Jack Dorsey said, Twitter was the perfect name for the program because "that's exactly what the product was." As cofounder Evan Williams added, "Who ever said things have to be useful?"

In the beginning, Twitter had a handful of accounts. By 2012, it had 200 million users with hundreds of millions of tweets posted every week. As of the publishing of this work, Twitter has more than 328 million users, sending out 500 million 140-character messages across the globe every single day. Contrary to the founders' early assumptions, Twitter has become quite useful and consequential. In fact, many people believe that it has not

Twitter has made it possible to share brief messages with other users all over the world within seconds, and it is popular with all kinds of users.

only revolutionized being able to keep in touch with everyone, it has also pro-foundly impacted the media, business, and politics. At its most useful, it is social networking with a purpose.

Twitter has opened up possibilities for citizen journalism. When a major event happens (anything from a natural disaster to a celebrity scandal), anyone with a smartphone or computer is mere seconds away from being able to share the news with the rest of the world. As Steven Johnson, author of *The Invention of Air*, once said of the platform, "This is what the naysayers fail to understand: it's just as easy to use Twitter to spread the word about a brilliant

10,000-word *New Yorker* article as it is to spread the word about your Lucky Charms habit."

Twitter has also opened a brand new door for communication between a company's employees (or CEOs) and its customers. Businesses can send messages to potential customers in real time. Customers can ask questions and voice complaints and compliments. Politicians and their constituents can also connect. Voters and other citizens can condemn or applaud their actions and argue among themselves.

There are many aims and goals you can accomplish online via social networks, and Twitter provides a way to engage both recreationally online and accomplish things with just a laptop, smartphone, or other internet-connected device on hand. Whether you are just on it for fun, as a fan or enthusiast of a particular scene or subculture, to network professionally, or to connect with others for political action, you, too, can learn what it's like to tweet with a purpose.

Chapter 1

Friends, Family, and Fun

There are many reasons to hop on Twitter and send a message to your friends, followers, and the Twitterverse in general. Whether you want to share your outrage at the local frozen yogurt shop for not carrying blueberry anymore, vent about a friend always showing up late, complain about a pop quiz at school, or rave about the last film you saw, you have a built-in audience. You can share your thoughts about your life in your posts, but you can do much more than that.

Making New Friends

Twitter is great for keeping in touch with your current friends, but it can also be a way to connect with new ones. Just as in real life, or "IRL," making friends takes effort. In the Twitterverse, making friends involves following accounts, retweeting, and frequently commenting on tweets. Don't wait to do this either. Users who tweet often tend to move on to something new very quickly. Once you have connected with someone on Twitter who amuses or interests you, the platform can feel far more engaging.

Twitter helps connect people with shared interests, like skateboarders, musicians, journalists, activists, fans, and more.

To find others who share your interests, use the Twitter search function. You can enter relevant terms—your high school's name, favorite writers or musicians, or anything you can think of—and see who comes up. If you use the advanced search, you can search using many different criteria. Remember that you cannot direct message (DM) people until they follow you, so start by replying to one of their tweets directly. Start a conversation, and keep it going.

File   Edit   View   Favorites   Tools   Help

THE BIRTH OF TWITTER

The Birth of Twitter

Like so many inventions of the tech era, Twitter came about because of a mixture of creativity, imagination, and patience. Officially, Twitter was born in the spring of 2006. The first tweet was a message from Jack Dorsey, one of the platform's cofounders. On March 21, 2006, he posted, "just setting up my twttr." (The program gained back a few of its vowels before it was finished.)

Dorsey and a number of other industry experts believed that Twitter would give people the chance to share their statuses in the world, much like texting, but to a broader audience and for little to no money. It was limited to 140 characters because it was originally designed to be a cell phone–based platform, and that was the limit that telecommunications carriers had at the time.

Where did using the # (hashtag) symbol come from? It was actually added to Twitter by the program's users. They wanted a way to identify others within a tweet or reply to a specific message, so they began putting the symbol before their usernames, also known as handles. Another addition was the use of "RT" before a message, to indicate it was being retweeted. It was first used by Twitter fans and then became part of the company's formatting a few years later.

In *Twitter for Dummies*, authors Laura Fitton, Anum Hussain, and Brittany Leaning write that Twitter has also proved useful "for couch-surfers, who have come to know interesting and accommodating people in different fields of expertise. Because Twitter helps people get to know one another on a more personal level, new friends can meet online and eventually come to interact offline."

Most younger users take advantage of mobile device technologies, like smartphones, to stay connected on social media networks, including Twitter.

Staying Entertained

Without doubt, one of the reason so many people like Twitter is that it allows them to be (somewhat) up close and personal with their favorite celebrities and cultural creators. Fans can follow their ups and downs and daily lives based on what they tweet. Musicians, authors, filmmakers, artists, and many other creative types have Twitter accounts now.

According to *Forbes* magazine, the top twenty accounts by follower count are run by celebrities. Fans may want to shout out their support for

Twitter Users: Who Are They?

Just who uses Twitter the most—and what are they using it to do? According to an infographic from HubSpot:

Active Users	312 million
Tweets sent per day	500 million
Percentage of Twitter users under the age of 18	16 percent
Percentage of Twitter users between 18 and 29	37 percent
Percentage of Twitter users between 30 and 64	37 percent
Percentage of Twitter users over the age of 65	10 percent
Peak times to use Twitter	Noon and 6 p.m.

Research from the American Press Institute has also shown that people use Twitter for a variety of reasons, including (from most popular to least popular):

- To be alerted to or find out more about breaking news
- To keep up with news in general
- To pass the time
- To tell others what they are doing or thinking about
- To see what others are talking about
- To keep in touch with friends and family
- To follow famous people
- To share news
- To network with others
- To follow trending topics

How many followers do celebrities have? The numbers are always changing, but in 2017, Katy Perry had one-hundred-and-two million, Justin Timberlake had sixty-two million, Lady Gaga had sixty-eight million, and former president Barack Obama had ninety-three million. President Donald Trump cracked twenty million followers just prior to his inauguration in January 2017.

recent performances. Critics might scold what they see as poor career decisions. Others might just want to ask questions or say hello.

Some television shows make the most out of Twitter too. Shows such as *Scandal*, *Pretty Little Liars*, *The Voice*, and *The Walking Dead* feature hashtags in the bottom corner of the TV screen while broadcasting. Searching for that specific hashtag can help fans gather online to discuss ideas, throw around theories, and make guarded guesses about what is going to happen next. Television producers love this kind of fan interaction, because it can go viral (spread fast) and is basically free.

Why do celebrities take time to post about what they ate, what movie role they hope to get, or what their next life goal is? In part, they do it for the same reason you do: to reach out and share a moment of life with other people. They also do it because they know it connects them to their audiences in a familiar way. Media consultant Kathleen Hessert told *Forbes*, "People want to know about celebrities as people. Those celebrities willing to share and do it authentically, those are the people who are going to engage fans in a way that builds their brand and perpetuates sponsors, and creates a kind of affinity that's hard to beat." Celebrities also recognize that regular tweets are a great way to send out news because especially dedicated fans are very likely to retweet their messages.

Remember, however, that there are a lot of fake accounts out there under famous names. Always look for the white and blue "verified" checkmark that signifies the account is legitimate. Also, even trusted accounts will sometimes have personal assistants and other staff tweet out things at times on their behalf, so it is good to take all tweets from superstars with a grain of salt.

Making the Most of a Post

You have a message to share, a question to ask, a request to make—and you have 140 characters to do it in (and remember—spaces count, but pictures, gifs, and attachments do not). How can you make the most of that very limited space? Here are a few tips from a variety of experts:

- Use strong verbs and minimize the adverbs and adjectives.
- Use shorter words, instead of longer more complex ones.
- Cut out unnecessary words such as "that" and "which."
- Take out personal pronouns.
- Use numerals, not numbers written out.
- If appropriate, you can put numbers as substitutes for parts of common words (for example, gr8 or b4).

Country musician Luke Bryan takes a picture with a fan, which can then be uploaded instantly onto the fan's (or Bryan's) Twitter timeline.

- Consider using abbreviations, acronyms, or shortened versions of words.
- Write your message and then go back and revise to cut it down.
- Get right to the point and be as succinct as possible.

If that's still not enough, you have other choices. You can include a link to a blog post where you have no word limits. You can do multiple tweets, too. The problem with that is that even if those two tweets are only seconds apart, they might be separated by half a dozen or more tweets on someone's timeline. If you decide to do this anyway, make sure to indicate that one tweet continues from another in some way.

MYTHS & FACTS

MYTH   Twitter is only for social networking.

FACT   *Time* magazine has called Twitter "the medium of the movement," deeming it one of the most important communication tools of its time. In 2008, Twitter users helped keep the world updated on what was happening during the terror attacks in Mumbai. The following year, Iranians used Twitter to organize protests against their government.

MYTH   Posting is done only for fun.

FACT   Recreation is a main reason many people go on Twitter, but it is far from the only reason. For many companies, celebrities, and politicians, Twitter is also an ideal marketing tool, and for activists and others it is valuable for advocating agendas and leading conversations on major issues.

MYTH   There are no concrete financial benefits to be gained from having a Twitter account.

FACT   While Twitter does not monetize followers and likes the way that YouTube does (with views and ad placement), you can stir up interest about your services or products or bring attention to a piece you have published. This could yield profitable page views or publicize YouTube videos or other media that can bring some profits.

15

Chapter 2

Keeping Current

Years ago, sharing news happened very slowly. Most messages went by letter, which could take weeks to arrive. The telegraph, invented in 1837, sped things up dramatically, but nothing like the world has at its fingertips now. Today's high-tech devices make it possible to keep up with events minutes or seconds after they happen or even live as they unfold. Twitter is one of the main platforms that has enabled this.

Not long ago, many people watched television news for local, state, national, and international coverage. Today people post the moment they experience or learn about something newsworthy. In early 2016, tens of thousands of people took part in #DrummondPuddleWatch in Newcastle, England. Yes, the puddle was big, and people were trying to find a way to cross it. But was it newsworthy?

Richard Jones, lecturer in journalism at the University of Huddersfield, told the Conversation, "The flow of information around the world is no longer just controlled by the Associated Press or Reuters—it's being tweeted, too ... [T]he first report of the raid which killed Osama bin Laden

The era of print news media has mostly passed. Many events are broadcast via Twitter before most news organizations with a digital presence catch wind of it.

in Pakistan came not from an official source but from a local IT consultant." Alecia Swasy, a professor of business journalism at the University of Illinois, told the *Illinois News Bureau*, "When a gunman started shooting at a Colorado move theater, the *Denver Post*'s first 24 hours of coverage was broken solely on social medial platforms like Twitter because the print edition was already on the delivery trucks."

Twitter has become not only an essential part of how people get their news, but one of the main reasons people use Twitter in the first place. It provides details in real time. As Lyse Doucet, chief international correspondent at the BBC, stated, "There is no question, if you are not on Facebook and Twitter, you are not getting the full story."

Unfortunately, not all posts on Twitter are accurate or appropriate. Users may post videos to Twitter that are too graphic or violate others' privacy. Celebrities like Jon Bon Jovi, Morgan Freeman, and Jeff Goldblum all have been incorrectly reported deceased via the platform.

As Irina Raicu, internet ethics program director at Santa Clara University, said to CIO, "[The] unfiltered aspect of social media has also led, on some platforms, to some very toxic exchanges —toxic enough to drive people completely out of the conversation. We have also seen that social media can enable the easy, fast, and widespread dissemination of misinformation."

Being Political

Twitter has made it easy for many people to follow political coverage. It can help you raise awareness of issues that might otherwise be overlooked and help to spread political messages as well as get feedback from others. It can help leaders organize actions like protests or meetups

Live events, such as the emergency response to this accident on a New York City street, can be followed in real time as they happen via Twitter.

or inspire people to get out and vote. This is especially true for more obscure or unknown causes or leaders. A local mayoral race or city council election might go under the radar: it takes only a few dedicated users tweeting to bring it to the attention of plenty of local people.

Thanks to Twitter, you can post about issues, passionately discuss topics with others, and find like-minded people you can relate to and communicate with. You can get involved with campaign events and share details, as well as help raise funds for a favorite candidate. You can also reach out and petition the government and any elected officials about issues that are important to you.

As journalist Vann Newkirk wrote about Twitter in the *Atlantic*, "Commentators and voters engage with the highest officeholders in the

A young woman takes a selfie to both announce and commemorate her voting in an election. A Twitter timeline can serve as a kind of scrapbook of important experiences.

world with candor, frankness—and often meanness and crassness—and sometimes even participate in real back-and-forth dialogue. This open dialogue … has also bolstered accountability and has caused the downfall of several politicians who were not so mindful of the new rules in play."

Virtually all members of Congress have their own Twitter accounts because, as Newkirk wrote, "A candidate without Twitter is a losing candidate." One of the most prolific fans of Twitter is President Donald Trump. His tweets were a large part of his 2016 presidential campaign because, as he

_ □ X

File   Edit   View   Favorites   Tools   Help

GOING VISUAL

Going Visual

Text-only tweets are only part of the Twitter experience. Many users were excited when Twitter acquired Periscope in January 2015. Periscope is a live-streaming video app that allows users to broadcast live video from anywhere. The video is then kept for up to twenty-four hours rather than disappearing at the end of the broadcast as with other apps. As Periscope's website states, "It may sound crazy, but we wanted to build the closest thing to teleportation. While there are many ways to discover events and places, we realized there is no better way to experience a place right now than through live video."

Periscope is a mobile app, so it lets you record spur-of-the-moment video when you get hit with inspiration. It allows you to share your moment on your timeline with others. Anyone watching can comment and ask you questions, creating a two-way interaction. Periscope truly creates that "you are there" feeling. In December 2016, the *Verge* reported that Periscope was fully integrated with the Twitter interface. Users did not necessarily have to even download the app, as the new Twitter feature was now "powered" by Telescope.

put it to Thought.co, "I like it [Twitter] because I can get also my point of view out there, and my point of view is very important to a lot of people that are looking at me."

Many of President Trump's tweets have upset people and set the Twitterverse afire with passionate discussion. Barry Burden, a political science professor at the University of Wisconsin–Madison told Thought.co, "[Trump's] aggressive and unconventional use of the platform generated news" even when those tweets turned out to "violate standard norms of campaigns by being uncivil, conspiratorial, or offensive."

Being Trolled

Being on Twitter exposes you to a lot of personal opinions. Some you might agree with. Others might annoy or even anger you. Remember that healthy debate and passionate discussion are fine but going online solely to argue with people and attack their perspectives is unhealthy. Doing so could earn you a reputation as a troll.

A troll is a person who intentionally encourages attacks and harassment online by starting arguments or posting offensive comments designed to provoke people. Trolls are not on Twitter in order to express opinions and have real discussions. They are not people who simply disagree with a position on an issue. Their purpose is primarily destructive.

What do you do if someone is trolling you on Twitter? First, don't follow their example and respond in anger. In other words, "Don't feed the trolls." Use Twitter's block and mute buttons to silence trolls' comments and to block them from your feed. As Brooke Magnanti wrote for the *Telegraph*, "It's OK to block people, it's OK to ignore them, it's OK to use your own online space however you like. This isn't censorship, and it doesn't deprive them of their platform to speak. It simply deprives them of making demands on your time and energy."

Depending on what this troll has been doing, consider reporting them to Twitter. In spring 2016, Twitter made that process easier. Users could collect multiple upsetting tweets and put them into a single complaint report.

Even if most of the people on your Twitter feed are not close friends you know in real life, any kind of harassment or piling-on via the platform can feel hurtful.

According to Twitter engineer Hao Tang, writing on Twitter's official blog, the company wants everyone to feel safe. Abusive behavior is against the company's rules so they added this new process. "This update makes it easier for you to provide us with more information about the extent of abuse and reduces the time it takes to do so," Tang wrote. Twitter makes it possible to instantly engage the world. Just make sure to bring along—and expect—good manners.

Chapter 3

Creating Community

Being on Twitter can offer more than just passive consumption of news or entertainment. It is also an incredible tool for helping you reach out and connect with others for encouragement, support, and activism. The platform can help people feel less alone by guiding them to like-minded people. Connecting with others who share one's gender identity, ethnic identity, or other commonalities is an important facet of Twitter. It can also help people to expand these networks, make alliances, and have polite and enlightening discussions with entirely different communities. Twitterers have used the service to help displaced families, victims of natural disasters, abuse victims, job seekers, animals in need, and even researchers who need people to take part in focus groups.

A Twitter account for a school band can keep friends and family appraised of upcoming performances, and help members stay connected while home or away.

File   Edit   View   Favorites   Tools   Help

MOST FAMOUS HASHTAGS AND OTHER RECORDS

Most Famous Hashtags and Other Records

Sometimes a hashtag will take off and be shared with thousands, or even millions. Some of the most well-known hashtags in Twitter's recent trending history include:

Hashtag	In response to
#JeSuisCharlie (Translates to "I Am Charlie")	2015 Paris terrorist attack on the publication *Charlie Hebdo*
#BlackLivesMatter	Police shootings of unarmed black citizens in many American cities
#MarriageEquality	The legalization of same-sex marriage
#RefugeesWelcome	Refugees fleeing wars in the Middle East
#Election2016	The election campaign between Hillary Clinton and Donald Trump
#Brexit	Britain's vote to quit the European Union, called Brexit (or "British Exit")

One of the most interesting tweets ever sent was in May 2009. It came from space! Astronaut Mike Massimino tweeted, "From orbit: Launch was awesome! I am feeling great, working hard, & enjoying the magnificent views, the adventure of a lifetime has begun!"

With a Little Tweet from My Friends

Although some people dismiss Twitter activism, there is little doubt it has helped people make a difference in many cases. For example, in 2014, the Ice Bucket challenge helped raise more than $115 million for the ALS Association and word spread of the movement via Twitter. More than 117

It's a good bet that at least some of the young people attending this Black Lives Matter march to protest the police shooting death of Paul O'Neal in Chicago, Illinois, first engaged with the #BLM movement via Twitter.

million people dumped buckets of ice water on their heads in exchange for donations for research into a cure for amyotrophic lateral sclerosis.

Perhaps one of the most prominent examples of a hashtag that has had real-world impact is #BlackLivesMatter. This Twitter campaign was first launched by activists Patrisse Cullors, Alicia Garza, and Opal Tometi in 2013. They were initially upset at the controversial exoneration of Florida gunman George

File   Edit   View   Favorites   Tools   Help

BEING BANNED FROM TWITTER

Being Banned from Twitter

What do journalist and author Charles Johnson and editor Milo Yiannopoulos have in common? Both of them have been banned from Twitter. Over the years, Twitter has consistently updated and revised its policies about abusive posts and "hateful conduct" used on their site. They have also worked hard to make it easier to report any type of abuse. Twitter uses a system of warnings and bans before taking the step of suspending someone permanently, as in the cases of Johnson and Yiannopoulos. Twitter's policy states, "We may suspend an account if it has been reported to us as violating our Rules surrounding abuse. When an account engages in abusive behavior, like sending threats to others or impersonating other accounts, we may suspend it temporarily or, in some cases, permanently."

Why was Yiannopoulos banned? "My suspension had made one thing clear," he said in an interview with NPR. "Twitter doesn't stand for free speech." Twitter countered, however, that the editor had been insulting people on the site for years, but when he turned his racist comments toward actress Leslie Jones (from *Saturday Night Live* and *Ghostbusters*), and also likely inspired a Twitter mob to chase her off the platform, it was the final straw.

As for Johnson, he did everything from publish the home addresses of reporters to asking for donations to "take out" a Black Lives Matter activist—essentially implying he wanted him killed. In response, Johnson wrote on GotNews.com, "Twitter doesn't seem to have a problem with people using their service to coordinate riots. But they do have a problem with the kind of journalism I do." Who else might be banned? According to some reports,

President Trump is being watched carefully on Twitter. The company is not afraid to ban him if he makes any explicit threats or violates their rules of behavior, such as harassment. As they have repeatedly stated, their policies apply to every user—including the president. While some people believe Trump should be suspended, others consider that a type of censorship that should be avoided at all costs. Ben Wizner, a free speech expert from the American Civil Liberties Union told the *New York Times*, "The world would be much worse off if Trump were kicked off Twitter. Before the election, during the election and after the election, we're all learning very important things about Trump from the way that he behaves through this unfiltered medium, so our discourse and our democracy would not benefit from removing that outlet for Trump."

Zimmerman, who was acquitted of murdering teenager Trayvon Martin in 2012. Their hashtag spread like wildfire, and inspired many African American people and their allies to march and protest, primarily against police violence in their communities, but also to highlight inequality in the justice system and society at large. Dozens of chapters have mobilized worldwide to form a powerful activist movement. Both #BlackLivesMatter and #BLM are commonly tweeted when incidents of police brutality occur.

By sharing important issues on a format such as Twitter, people are able to share stories faster and spread them faster than any single journalist possibly could. As Corey Smock wrote on Likeable.com, "Although some may refer to this movement as a form of Slacktivism, there is no denying that this Twitter activity fueled a central focus for the international news media. The millions who are joined across the world certainly had more influence than a single report churned out by a concerned journalist."

Use Twitter to do more than follow and comment. Use it to get involved in a cause or charity. Plan an event, or at least, help promote one. Clicking on a screen is just one part of making the planet a nicer place, but it cannot end there. Real world actions may start with a retweet, but they need not end there.

Making Friends—and Followers

As American businessman Dick Costolo phrases it, "One of the things that amazes me about Twitter is the way it utterly eradicates artificial barriers to communication. Things like status, geopolitics, and so on keep people from talking to one another. Those go away in Twitter," he added. "You see exchanges that would never happen anywhere else."

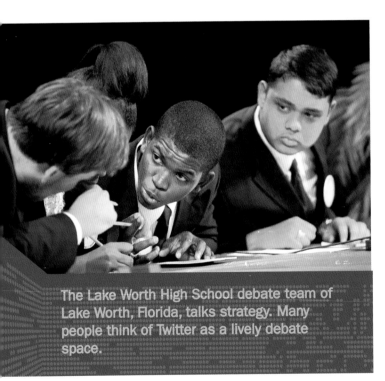

The Lake Worth High School debate team of Lake Worth, Florida, talks strategy. Many people think of Twitter as a lively debate space.

Knowing how to find specific groups that you want to communicate with frequently requires a combination of searching online and then, once you're following people, asking them for additional profiles. Also, try just putting a hashtag symbol in front of some of the most common words involved in your interest or cause.

For example, for people with a variety of disabilities, the following hashtags are used:

- #TheBarriersWeFace
- #WheelchairLife

- #ActuallyAutistic
- #DisabilityTooWhite
- #GetYourBellyOut (ostomy awareness)
- #AbleismExists
- #DisaBodyPosi (Disability Body Positive)
- #ShowMeYourPump (diabetes awareness)
- #DeafTalent
- #InvisibleIllness
- #ServiceDog

If you are interested in connecting with people in the LGBTQ community, on the other hand, you can check out hashtags like:

- #bornthisway
- #loveislove
- #Pride
- #gayrights
- #transrights
- #itgetsbetter
- #stopbullying
- #suicideprevention
- #equality

Another suggestion comes from the authors of *Twitter for Dummies*. They suggest putting a mission statement on your account that lets people understand more about you. Author Laura Fitton suggests a template that reads,

> (Your username) is where (type of people) can find (value offered on your account)."

Once you have connected with others, you can follow each other, check out links, and work together to get more involved in your community.

Chapter 4

Promoting You

Beyond using Twitter as a tool to help others, it is also a great platform to promote yourself. You can use it to reach out to potential employers or get information about a particular industry. If you are a creative person just starting out—a musician, journalist, author, or video editor, among many others—there is no substitute for the kind of reach Twitter can provide. You can put your posts to work promoting whatever it is you want to share with the world, whether it be your blog, YouTube vlog, website, or actual products or services.

Getting Results—and Jobs

Twitter can help connect you to companies quicker than sending an email or letter. In some cases, customer service might respond to questions or complaints in a matter of hours, instead of days or weeks. Companies can track their most loyal customers and use the information to predict upcoming consumer trends. Advertising is quick and available 24/7. A Twitter storm (a flurry of complaints or negative comments posted about a company or a

If you have a small business, or you are a freelancer or a creative professional, Twitter can serve as a very useful tool to market your services, advertise your skills, and land fans and clients.

product by many users) can occasionally even make a company change its policies or make internal changes.

The platform also gives you the opportunity to watch for job openings and to reach out about getting hired—or at least get to know a few people that might make that possible. Luke Westaway, senior editor at CNET, told the *Guardian*,

> Twitter more or less got me a job. Back in 2009 I was blogging my socks off and trying to break into tech reporting, and

Twitter let me find the journos who'd already made it, follow them, observe their habits and, when I was feeling especially courageous, chime in with polite comments ... I used Twitter to get to know people I dreamed of working with, brag my way into industry events, and it gave me a helicopter view of a pretty cliquey industry that I couldn't have achieved otherwise. I remember using Twitter to take a journo up on a food voucher offer they tweeted, then when we'd sorted it out over DMs, asking for an email address to pitch freelance to. Now I work with that guy at CNET!

Twitter can serve as one of several social media platforms one can use to accomplish things, whether they entail business or pleasure.

"Hey, Would You Like to Check Out ... "

Twitter can be a helpful way to get the word out about whatever you are working on. Clearly, 140 characters is not enough to say much, so instead just post a little update or mention a sale or special promotion and then link to the website where the details can be found.

— □ X

File   Edit   View   Favorites   Tools   Help

 TWITTER GRAMMAR

Twitter Grammar

Is the abbreviated writing and use of acronyms used with social media sites like Twitter helping language evolve—or devolve? It depends on who you ask. There are a number of educators who believe that the compressed language most social media sites feature is teaching students to ignore rules of grammar and leave out important words. Professor David Abulafia from Cambridge University says that these new habits are sending students' essay skills "down the plug hole." However, a study release by the Pew Research Center's Internet & American Life Project along with the National Writing Project reported that 78 percent of high school teachers believe that today's digital technologies "encourage student creativity and personal expression."

In addition, virtually all teachers polled agreed that these same technologies give students the chance to share their writing with a large and varied audience. Joel Malley, a teacher, told ABC News, "It creates a culture of creativity. They [students] know they will be watched and viewed. It won't just sit in a closet." Kristen Purcell, the Pew Center's director of research added, "Most teachers told us they wouldn't consider texting or tweeting as formal writing, in the strict sense, but they used the term 'pre-writing.' Students start to express their thoughts and that means students are writing more and they see that as a plus."

The report isn't all positive, however. Studies do show that frequent use of "chatspeak" like that used on social media sites can lead students to use poor spelling and grammar, so extra attention has to be paid to the old standards, even when using the most modern technology.

Family Online Safety Institute (FOSI)
400 7th Street NW, Suite 506
Washington, DC 20004
(202) 775-0158
Website: http://www.fosi.org
Twitter: @FOSI
The FOSI focuses on online safety for all ages. It partners with companies
    such as Amazon and Yahoo! and hosts an annual conference about
    online safety.

Social Media Club (SMC)
Global Headquarters
PO Box 14881
San Francisco, CA 94114-0881
Website: http://socialmediaclub.org
Twitter: @socialmediaclub
The SMC hosts conventions around the world that explore key issues
    surrounding social media and communication.

Social Media Lab
10 Dundas Street East, #1002
Toronto, ON M5B 2G9
Canada
Website: http://socialmedialab.ca
Twitter: @SMLabTO
The Social Media Lab is a multi- and interdisciplinary research laboratory at
    the Ted Rogers School of Management at Ryerson University in Toronto,
    Canada. The lab studies how social media is changing the ways peo-
    ple communicate, disseminate information, conduct business, and
    form communities.

Twitter
1355 Market Street, Suite 900
San Francisco, CA 94103
Website: https://about.twitter.com/company
Twitter: @Twitter
This website details what Twitter is about, plus it has links to the official
	Twitter blog, which is focused on "keeping you connected to everything
	from Twitter."

Word of Mouth Marketing and Advertising (WOMMA)
200 E. Randolph Street, Suite 5100
Chicago, IL 60601
(312) 577-7610
Website: http://womma.org
Twitter: @womma
WOMMA is an association dedicated to word of mouth and social media
	marketing.

Websites

Because of the changing nature of internet links, Rosen Publishing has
developed an online list of websites related to the subject of this book.
This site is updated regularly. Please use this link to access this list:

http://www.rosenlinks.com/DIL/Tweet

FOR FURTHER READING

Espejo, Roman. *What is the Impact of Twitter?* New York, NY: Greenhaven Press, 2013.

Gilbert, Sara. *The Story of Twitter*. Mankato, MN: Creative Education, 2015.

Henneberg, Susan. *Twitter Safety and Privacy: A Guide to Microblogging*. New York, NY: Rosen Publishing, 2013.

Hepperman, Christine. *Twitter: The Company and Its Founders*. Minneapolis, MN: Abdo Publishing Company, 2012.

Kamberg, Mary-Lane. *Evan Williams, Biz Stone, Jack Dorsey, and Twitter (Internet Biographies)*. New York, NY: Rosen Publishing, 2013.

Kent, Germany. *You Are What You Tweet: Harness the Power of Twitter to Create a Happier, Healthier Life*. Culver City, CA: Star Stone Press, 2015.

Kielburger, Craig, and Marc Mielburger. *My Grandma Follows Me on Twitter: And Other First-World Problems We're Lucky to Have*. Toronto, Ontario: Me to We Publishing, 2014.

Lamont, Ian. *Twitter in 30 Minutes: How to Connect with Interesting People, Write Great Tweets, and Find Information that's Relevant to You*. Newton, MA: In 30 Minutes Guides, 2016.

Mattern, Joanne. *Twitter*. Minneapolis, MN: Checkerboard Library/Abdo Publishing, 2017.

Scott, Celicia. *Twitter: How Jack Dorsey Changed the Way We Communicate*. Broomall, PA: Mason Crest Publishers, 2014.

BIBLIOGRAPHY

Carlson, Nicholas. "The Real History of Twitter." *Business Insider*, April 13, 2011. http://www.businessinsider.com/how-twitter-was-founded -2011-4.

Chamberlain, Craig. "How Has Twitter Changed News Coverage?" Illinois News Bureau. October 22, 2015. https://news.illinois.edu/blog /view/6367/267046.

Cresci, Elena. "12 Ways Twitter Changed Our Lives." *Guardian*, March 21, 2016. https://www.theguardian.com/technology/2016/mar/21 /12-ways-twitter-changed-our-lives-10th-birthday.

Fitton, Laura, Anum Hussain, and Brittany Leaning. *Twitter for Dummies*. Hoboken, NJ: John Wiley & Sons, 2015.

Greenberg, Andy. "Why Celebrities Twitter." *Forbes*, March 3, 2009. https:// www.forbes.com/2009/03/03/twitter-celebrities-privacy-technology -internet_twitter.html.

Henry, Julie. "Art of Essay-Writing Damaged by Twitter and Facebook, Cambridge Don Warns." *Telegraph*, January 20, 2013. http://www .telegraph.co.uk/technology/social-media/9813109/Art-of -essay-writing-damaged-by-Twitter-and-Facebook-Cambridge -don-warns.html.

Kottasova, Ivana. "The Top Hashtag of the Year Had Nothing to Do with Donald Trump." CNN, December 6, 2016. http://money.cnn .com/2016/12/06/technology/twitter-top-events-hashtags-2016.

Krauskopf, Lewis. "Celebrities Tell Followers to #GetCovered with Obamacare." *Huffington Post*, October 2, 2013. http://www.huffingtonpost.com/2013/10/02/getcovered-obamacare -celebrities-_n_4029727.html.

Lee, Aaron. "Twitter Makes It Easier to Report Trolls' Abusive Tweets." *IT Pro*, April, 26, 2016. http://www.itpro.co.uk/strategy/26421 /twitter-makes-it-easier-to-report-trolls-abusive-tweets.

Lee, Dave. "How Twitter Changed the World, Hashtag-by-Hashtag." BBC News, November 7, 2013. http://www.bbc.com/news/technology.

Magnati, Dr. Brooke. "How to Deal with Twitter Trolls." *Telegraph*, May 20, 2013. http://www.telegraph.co.uk/women/womens-life/10068940/ How-to-deal-with-Twitter-trolls.html.

Manjoo, Farhad. "Twitter Has the Right to Suspend Donald Trump. But It Shouldn't." *New York Times,* December 14, 2016. https://www .nytimes.com/2016/12/14/technology/twitter-has-the-right-to -suspend- donald-trump-but-it-shouldnt.html?_r=0.

Marie Claire. "What Is Periscope? What You Need to Know about Twitter's New App." June 16, 2015. http://www.marieclaire .co.uk/entertainment/technology/what-is-periscope-what-you-need -to-know-about-twitter-s-new-app-71206.

Murse, Tom. "How Social Media Has Changed Politics." ThoughtCo. August 23, 2016. https://www.thoughtco.com/how-social-media-has -changed-politics-3367534 Retrieved March 31, 2017.

Newkirk, Vann. "The American Idea in 140 Characters." *Atlantic*, March 24, 2016. https://www.theatlantic.com/politics/archive/2016/03 /twitter-politics-last-decade/475131.

Newton, Casey. "You Can Now Broadcast Live Video from the Twitter App." Verge, December 14, 2016. http://www.theverge.com/2016/12/14 /13942840/twitter-live-video-periscope-integration.

Restle, Hope. "Here's Who Is Using Twitter around the World." *Business Insider*, June 30, 2015. http://www.businessinsider.com/who -uses-twitter-2015-6.

Selyukh, Alina. "What Does It Take to Get Permanently Banned from Twitter?" NPR, July 20, 2016. http://www.npr.org/sections/alltechconsidered/2016/07/20/486738705/what-does-it-take-to-get-permanently-banned-from-twitter.

"Six Ways Twitter Has Changed the World." Conversation, March 18, 2016. http://theconversation.com/six-ways-twitter-has-changed-the-world-56234.

Smock, Corey. "How Twitter Has Changed Journalism Forever." Likeable Media, August 28, 2014. http://www.likeable.com/blog/2014/08/how-twitter-has-changed-journalism-forever.

Stern, Joanna. "Social Media Makes for Better Student Writing, Not Worse, Teachers Say." ABC News, July 16, 2013. http://abcnews.go.com/Technology/social-media-makes-student-writing-worse-teachers/story?id=19677570.

Trimarchi, Maria. "5 Myths About Twitter." HowStuffWorks.com, July 24, 2009. http://electronics.howstuffworks.com/tech-myths/5-myths-about-twitter.htm.

Williams, Rhiannon. "What Is Twitter's New Periscope App?" Telegraph, March 28, 2015. http://www.telegraph.co.uk/technology/2015/12/010/what-is-twitters-new-periscope-app.

INDEX

A

activists, 15, 24, 27, 28, 29
ALS Association, 27
artists and musicians, 8, 10, 32, 36

B

bin Laden, Osama, 16–17
#BlackLivesMatter (#BLM), 26, 27, 28, 29
blogs, 14, 33, 37
#Brexit, 26
business communication, 6, 36

C

celebrities, 4, 5, 10, 11, 12, 15, 18
citizen journalism, 5–6
Clinton, Hillary, 26
comedians, 36

D

disabilities, 30–31
direct messaging (DM), 8, 34
Dorsey, Jack, 4, 9

E

#Election2016, 26
email, 4, 32, 34

F

Facebook, 4, 18

H

hashtags, 9, 12, 26, 27, 30–31
hateful content, 28–29

I

Ice Bucket Challenge, 27

J

#JeSuisCharlie, 26
jobs, finding, 32–34
Johnson, Charles, 28–29
Jones, Leslie, 28

L

LGBTQ community, 31

M

#MarriageEquality, 26
Martin, Trayvon, 27, 29
misinformation, 18
mission statements, 31
Massimino, Mike, 26
multiple tweets, 14

N

news, dissemination of, 16–18, 22–23, 29

P

Periscope, 21
politics, 5, 6, 15, 18, 20–22
pre-writing, 35

R

#RefugeesWelcome, 26
reporting abuse, 22, 28
retweeting, 7, 9, 12, 30, 36, 38

S

self promotion, 32–34, 35–36
social media, 4, 6, 17, 18, 35, 37
social networking, 5, 38
student writing, 35

T

television shows, 12
trolls, 22–23
Trump, Donald, 11, 21–22, 26, 29
Twitter
    birth of, 4, 9
    blocking on, 22
    and grammar, 35
    making friends on, 7–9, 30–31
    making the most of posts, 12–14
    as a marketing tool, 15, 32–34, 36
    myths and facts, 15
    name origin, 4
    policies, 23, 28–29
    as a political tool, 5, 6, 15, 18, 20–22
    reasons to use, 11
    as a tool for activism, 15, 24, 27, 29
    top-followed accounts, 10, 11, 12
    user statistics, 4, 11
    video streaming on, 21
Twitter storm, 32

V

verified accounts, 12

W

Williams, Evan, 4

Y

Yiannopoulos, Milo, 28–29
YouTube, 15, 32

Z

Zimmerman, George, 27, 29

About the Author

Tamra Orr is the author of many nonfiction and educational books for readers of all ages. She graduated from Ball State University with a degree in education and English and has spent her life learning about the world. She lives with her family in the Pacific Northwest where she researches and writes during her work hours and goes camping and writes letters in her free time. Tamra Orr is the author of *Creating Multimedia Presentations, I Have Been Shamed on the Internet. Now What?* and *What Degree Do I Need to Pursue a Career in Business?*

Photo Credits

Cover, p. 1 (left to right) karelnoppe/Shutterstock.com, antoniodiaz /Shutterstock.com, blackday/Shutterstock.com, Portrait Images Asia by Nonwarit/Shutterstock.com; p. 5 Sattalat Phukkum/Shutterstock.com; p. 8 Anna Om/iStock/Thinkstock; p. 10 George Rudy/Shutterstock.com; p. 13 Debby Wong/Shutterstock.com; p. 17 Seraficus/iStock/Thinkstock; pp. 18-19 Education Images/Universal Images Group/Getty Images; p. 20 Hero Images/Getty Images; p. 23 © iStockphoto.com/Jeremyiswild; pp. 24-25 Monkeybusinessimages/iStock/Thinkstock; p. 27 NurPhoto /Getty Images; p. 30 ZUMA Press Inc/Alamy Stock Photo; p. 33 Chaay Tee /Shutterstock.com; p. 34 Twin Design/Shutterstock.com; p. 37 Ermolaev Alexander/Shutterstock.com; cover and interior pages (pixels) © iStock photo.com/suprun.

Design: Nicole Russo-Duca; Layout: Raúl Rodriguez; Editor: Phil Wolny; Photo Research: Karen Huang

DATE DUE

PRINTED IN U.S.A